UNTOLD STORIES OF THE NHS

Untold Stories of the NHS

Edited by Kim Moore

Manchester
Metropolitan
University

Manchester Metropolitan University gratefully acknowledges assistance from the Arts and Humanities Research Council.

This project was delivered in partnership with Lime Arts, NHS England, Manchester University NHS Foundation Trust and Manchester UNESCO City of Literature.

Contents

Introduction | *Kim Moore*   vii

Myths and Legends of Trafford Hospital |
Amanda Jordan & Kim Moore   1

My First NHS Hospital | *Anjali Santhakumar*   3

Last Offices | *Kim Moore*   7

The Birthplace of the NHS | *Katie Kirkham*   9

This is What I Say | *Gillian Lambert*   13

Why Trafford? | *Michelle Davies*   15

Covid Diary | *Martha Sheen*   17

First Day at Work | *Amanda Jordan*   25

The Porters | *Kim Moore*   27

Shine like a Diamond | *Monica Donnelly*   31

The Stethoscope | *Anjali Santhakumar*   35

Who You Gonna Call | *Thomas Lee*   37

Words of Wisdom | *Angela Reeve*   39

Ebb and Flow | *Anna Jerram*   41

The Moral Battle of HR | *Amanda Jordan*   47

CONTENTS

The Nightingale Hospital | *Asma Ahmed*   49

A Small Part in a Big Machine | *Elaine Brogan*   51

Christmas at Radio Wishing Well | *Gillian Lambert*   53

The Importance of Empathy | *Mike Ainsworth*   55

I Remember | *Anjali Santhakumar*   59

The Voice | *Gillian Lambert*   61

The Laminator Speaks | *Michelle Davies*   63

Two Doctors | *Anonymous*   65

Sarah's Story | *Anonymous*   69

Love You | *Martha Sheen*   73

The Cardiac Arrest | *Anjali Santhakumar*   75

The Visiting Duchess | *Jane Gigner-Hollies & Kim Moore* 77

Five Minutes with Jakub Dosa | *Jakub Dosa*   79

Dom's Story | *Domonnie Francis*   81

What I Know | *Thomas Lee & Kim Moore*   83

About the Project   85
About the Editor   87

Introduction

Kim Moore

Writer-in-Residence

EVERY TUESDAY SINCE JANUARY, I've been working as a Writer-in-Residence at Trafford General Hospital. In the first two months of the residency, this involved sitting at a table in the Bevan restaurant for the day, and talking to members of staff who showed a flicker of interest in the giant banner and the postcards on the table, which asked the question, 'Do you remember your first day at work?'

/

I wake up at 6am, get dressed and am out of the house and on my bike by 6.20am. I am half-asleep still. I don't have a cup of tea. I don't really want to wake up properly until I'm on the train. I like the feeling of falling through time and space, down the hill from my house to the station, through How Tun Woods and down, down, along Oxford Street, and down again to pick up Abbey Road before freewheeling into Barrow train station, still over 100 miles away from Trafford General Hospital.

/

Why did I want to be a Writer-in-Residence at a hospital? Mostly because I find people fascinating, and especially people who do what I think of as 'real jobs'. But I also find institutions fascinating, having spent my whole life as part of one institution or another. All institutions are made of the people that work inside them, but this is true for some more than others.

/

It's April, and the sun has come out, so instead of taking the train from Manchester Oxford Road to Urmston, I get off at Deansgate and cycle the six miles along the canal. The geese are out in force with their goslings, hissing as I pass by. I get a fly in my eye and have to stop to blink it away. One particularly enthusiastic goose nearly dashes me off the path and into the hedge, but I manage to just keep my balance and wobble past. My back aches from the weight of my bag. I wonder if the books I'm lugging around are really necessary.

/

When I first started this project, I imagined I would run a series of workshops that staff would attend. They would write their own stories and poems and send them to me. I might give them feedback, editorial suggestions and we would have a conversation about their piece of work. They would send a finished version, which I would then collate into an anthology.

This turned out to be true, but it was just one of the many ways that staff engaged with the project. Sometimes someone would tell me a story, and I would feel a kind of pressure building up in my brain, and I would know that I had to find somewhere to sit and write a poem, using what they'd told me. Sometimes I sat and just recorded them talking, and then typed up the transcript. I made rules for myself – I could move material around and delete things, but I couldn't add anything new.

Each person, each story, each poem invented its own

methodology. Seeing them together now, I realise I've been working in a strange, hybrid way – moving between writer and editor, writer and mentor, writer and journalist.

/

In the canteen, a woman comes up to me and tells me she has worked at Trafford for twenty years. She's in a rush, on her way back to the ward after her lunch break and has that air of someone who is running late. But she also moves as if the ground under her feet is slightly hot, as if she can't stay still too long. She says that if she was rich, she would work here for free, that the NHS saved her life, that she'd do anything for this hospital. I ask her if she'd write something, or if she'd like to come to a workshop. She says she would love to tell her story, and she will send me something. I think she really meant it, but I don't see her again. Still, I think about her words a lot.

/

The final two months of the residency are spent running workshops, one in the morning and one in the afternoon. I work with domestic assistants, nurses, a consultant, a nursing assistant, therapeutic activities co-ordinators, students, mental health workers, someone from Human Resources and volunteers from the hospital radio. I send out an email each week to the staff mailing list and invite people that I meet in the restaurant. The workshops are free, and I try to make a space where staff can just come and write and be creative.

/

I ask them to write for two minutes without thinking. I ask them to take a sentence for a walk. I ask them to write about a conversation that is memorable to them. I ask them to write about their first day. I ask them to write about an object that they use at work that is important to them. I ask them to take the phrase 'I remember' and finish it. I ask them to tell me what they know.

/

I cannot write about what happens in the workshops, because what happens in the workshop stays in the workshop. I can say that a writing workshop is both a place of safety, and a place of vulnerability, that both of these things can be true. The workshop is the great leveller – although it would be naïve to say it makes invisible the hierarchical structure of an organisation such as the NHS, it does cut across it, slices through it as if it is nothing.

/

I go and say hello to Angela and Jakub in the Estates and Catering Office. 'Hello, Dr Kim!' they exclaim. They always sound pleased to see me – I think this gentle mockery means they like me, and as it's the only time I've been called Dr Kim with regular occurrence, I decide to enjoy it. Angela hides a menu that she's looking at and says, 'It's a steakhouse. I thought you were a veggie!' Apparently, being a poet makes it more likely that I'm vegetarian. Jakub offers to take me to the porter's office. As we are walking down the corridor, he says, 'If they won't co-operate, just come back.' I feel slightly alarmed. 'Have you told them that I'm coming to speak to them?' I ask. Jakub waves a hand airily. 'Oh, no, it will be fine.'

/

Towards the end of the project, photographer Chris Saunders is commissioned to take photographs of the participants. Whilst the original plan was to photograph twelve participants who had engaged with the project, this does not quite reflect what this residency has been like – and there was no way I could have narrowed it down to twelve. Instead there are eighteen participants photographed, with a further two who either did not want to be photographed or were away whilst the photographs were being taken. There is something beautiful and haunting about each photograph, something hidden and revealed.

/

The porter's office is quite small, and lined with chairs. There's a basic kitchen for them to make their lunch if they want, and it's opposite the post room of the hospital. Our conversation is slightly awkward and feels stilted. I ask them if they can remember their first day at work. The youngest porter, Reece, says that on his first day, he had to help move a body. Then the person he was moving the body with got called out of the room, and he was left there alone. He thought they were playing a joke on him, that the 'corpse' would sit up, climb down from the bed. But it was no joke. The body stayed still.

/

Part way through the residency, my dad is rushed into hospital with internal bleeding. He is in a different hospital of course, in a different part of the country, but I don't panic as much as I might have. I think about the staff that I've met here. I would trust my dad with any of them.

I miss one week of the residency. My dad is still in hospital. I travel to see him and stay at the hospital all day. He is waiting for an operation, having bag after bag of blood pumped through him. There's nothing to do but wait. Sometimes it feels like a scene from a horror film. I feel like I'm going to have a panic attack. I don't know if I'm not panicking enough, or if I need to be calm.

/

I write a poem about the porters, and take a hard copy in. When I see one of the porters in the canteen, I pounce and ask if I can show it to him. He agrees to take it down to the porter's office to show the others. Later, another porter comes up to me in the canteen and shakes my hand, says I got it exactly right. This means more to me than anything. I think that if I do nothing else in this residency, that would have made it worth it.

/

I wanted to write about scaffolding, but every time I went onto the building site with my dad, I could feel it change around me. By being a woman in this hyper-masculine environment I changed it, so could never 'see' it, in the way it should be seen, or at least the way I wanted it to be seen. The porter's office felt like a similar place. There are jokes that will not be told whilst I am there, and stories that will never be written down.

/

I am back in Trafford. My dad might be discharged tomorrow, if he continues to improve. I feel shaky as I walk through the hospital doors. The feelings of helplessness and panic I felt as I waited for the NHS to save my father rise up again. I have to stop and slow my breathing down whilst pretending I'm reading something on my phone. I see one of the porters on the corridor and he stops to have a chat. He asks how my dad is. He puts his hand on my shoulder, and asks me if I'm alright.

/

One of the turning points in the residency is meeting Martha, a nurse in her twenties. She reminds me of one of my nieces, although I don't tell her that. She seems so full of life and as if she is always about to break into a smile. She tells me that she kept a diary throughout Covid and that I can have it for the project if I like. The first time I read the diary, it suddenly feels as if the residency is a living, breathing animal, and I have just found the skeleton to keep it upright.

/

The diary has a brown cover, with flowers on the front. It's a notebook really, with looped handwriting filling the first third of its pages. I walk down the hospital corridor and start to read. It is what I've done since childhood, reading whilst walking, because I couldn't bear to put down a book. I can walk up and down stairs, and around objects whilst reading. I start to cry as I'm reading the diary. It is something about the very factual statements. The recording of death, that of course death mattered, and yet she has to carry on, through something that would stop most people in their tracks. She turns up for work, again and again.

/

This is just a very small account, or one version of what it has been like to be in the hospital. When I think of the NHS, I think of something that takes care of us all, but also something we must take care of in return. Staff who work within the NHS are also patients of it, they have family who use it. In this way, we are all connected to each other. The strength of our NHS, on this 75th anniversary and beyond, lies in the staff who work within it, who despite extraordinary challenges continue to give of themselves, and give themselves over to a life of service.

I hope you find moments of empathy, connection and kinship in these pages, and enjoy meeting some of our ordinary, extraordinary NHS staff.

Myths and Legends of Trafford Hospital

Amanda Jordan & Kim Moore

Radio Station Manager & HR

Once upon a time, in the middle of the night, when the owls flew with silent wings and the moon was a spent coin in the sky, a group of hospital staff gathered in the shadow of the clock tower. It's said that some were junior doctors, years into their training, whilst some had barely begun. And some were nurses, who had already seen everything there was to see in all the world, but had never seen an old-style Mini in the service lift. And so they all swore an oath to try, and they drove the Mini up to the clock tower, and some people say that all those who swore the oath climbed inside, and some say that nobody did, that it was driven by a shadow or a ghost. When it entered the hospital, it kept going, along the corridor, into the lift, and then along the first-floor corridor. Some say that if you stand by the clock tower at midnight, at a certain time of year, when the first frost has settled on the trees, and winter is a constant thought in the mind of the sky, you might hear the sound of the engine of that Mini, or even a kind of laughter on the wind.

My First NHS Hospital

Anjali Santhakumar

Consultant

I WAS WALKING INTO the unknown. I had trained and learnt my trade well in India. Pursuing higher training in the UK, my first clinical attachment in the NHS was on the Western Isles, which according to a casual acquaintance at the time was the Britain of 50 years ago. I had no idea what Britain was like 50 years ago – or even at that time – and remember thinking how this piece of information was useless to me! Information about the institution of the NHS was, of course, more useful and it was described as *the* place to work if you are doing medicine in the UK.

I arrived on Stornoway in a frightfully small aircraft, too close to the wide expanse of water for comfort. However, with a population of around 6000, the airport transit would be the quickest I would ever know. I landed in what could only be described as freezing horizontal rain. I quickly realised this was going to be a constant feature and went to one of the few clothes shops on the island and purchased the thickest fleece-lined jacket I could find. I wore this dreary beige jacket during the entirety of my initial six months stint as a clinical attachee and the subsequent six months I spent on this beautiful island as a senior house officer.

The hospital was small and welcoming; most of my patients had the same surname so that could be confusing or helpful depending on how you chose to see it. I was one of three or so junior medical doctors in the hospital. My circle of friends at the time on this island was made up of the hospital pharmacist, the podiatrist and a couple of doctors. In our spare time, we took long walks and discovered the beautiful beaches and the open barren landscapes together. People we encountered on these trips were on occasion our patients later on. I learnt quickly that everything shuts down on the Isles on Sundays. Our consultant on a rare occasion would give us a lift in his car to fetch groceries from the local shop after work, saving us all a few hundred steps.

I learnt to cook in the staff accommodation with other novice cooks and the local fire brigade used to respond to false fire alarms on a regular basis. The local joke was that the fire brigade didn't rush if the call was from the hospital staff quarters!

There were clinics on nearby islands where even smaller planes landed directly on the beach and bad weather meant an overnight stay.

I put my newly gained Western-styled communication skills, courtesy of the UK entry examination, to good use. As a clinical attachee, I matched my significant Indian medical experience with the more junior doctors who had relatively lesser clinical experience, (but with significantly more social and communication skills than I), and we made a good team. I learnt the nuances and vagaries of the local population, and the NHS healthcare, and slowly gained the trust and confidence of the senior medical team. I saw my first snowfall with a sense of wonder through the large clear windows of the medical ward here. I learnt how to winch down from a helicopter in case anyone on the local sea ferry needed medical attention.

Through all the hard work it slowly hit me that for the first time, I was enjoying my medicine. I realised in amazement I was delivering classic textbook medical care. Treating patients with exactly the treatment recommended in the hefty medical textbooks I had to devour during my training.

I had spent part of my medical training in remote areas of rural India with limited resources, trying to deliver the best possible care but not always succeeding.

Here I was among unbridled amazing care, not burdened by costs, availability or affordability. What joy!

To the eyes of this young doctor, the NHS was amazing. In addition to the exemplary medical treatment, what particularly stood out was the high level of support the elderly were getting on the wards. The physiotherapy, the occupational therapy and the social resources available were truly splendid. The concept of getting the homes of patients ready prior to their discharge was alien to me and I often wondered at the time whether the patients using the NHS realised just how lucky they were to be taken care of by this amazing institution.

I have now worked across an abundance of NHS hospitals progressing to an NHS consultant of many years standing now, and I still think the NHS is amazing and *the* place to work. I will always treasure memories of my first ever NHS hospital and would not have had it any other way. My only regret is that I did not attempt my driving test on that beautiful island with a single roundabout!

Edited by Saanvi Hari

Last Offices

Kim Moore

Writer-in-Residence

AND SO WE BEGAN
    to think differently
      of death

when it was common as a song
    as close to us as a shadow
      as insistent as applause

each time it visited the ward
    it altered everything
      in a wind of its own making

made all our well-known rituals disappear
    and so in the absence of ritual
      we made our own

knowing there was nobody now
    to unzip the body bags
      no embalming to raise up

the beloved to the surface once again
    and so we became obsessed
      by what happened after

our last offices
    after the cleaning-washing-drying
        we dressed them

as if they were our fathers or our mothers
    our sons and daughters
        sisters, brothers

lipstick for a woman whose make-up
    was always perfect
        and for the man

whose wife wanted him to smell
    only of himself – a dab of aftershave
        behind each ear

and in the soft place of the throat
    a Man United shirt for the football fan
        we sat and held a hand

waited for a last breath
    for that was our job
        we dressed them

in the mind's eye
    in the heart
        in a memory of a memory

The Birthplace of the NHS

Katie Kirkham

Domestic Assistant

My name is Katie Kirkham and I'm a domestic assistant at Trafford Hospital. I've worked here for around thirteen, fourteen years. When I first started, I never intended to work here for this long. I'd done a few other things, but was between jobs, and one of my friends who works here said to me, 'Oh, they're looking for domestics at the hospital. I think you'll fit right in.' And when I asked her what a domestic does, she goes, 'Oh, it's a cleaner.' I said, 'Oh, I don't want to be a cleaner.' But then I thought, I need a job, I'll give it a go.

It was supposed to be a stopgap until I found something else. But when I started, I thought, 'Wow, this is quite nice actually. I'm enjoying it.' And it's not just cleaning. There's more to it than that. You're interacting with patients. I was quite surprised that I was enjoying it – and then fourteen years later, I'm still here.

I've done a variety of different jobs over the years. I've done shop work, I've done restaurant work, I've worked in a takeaway, a chemist. Nothing that lasted too long, until I came here! I think it helps that we've got good staff. It helps when you've got good people in the ward. They're all nice, friendly people. We all get on with one another. We all look out for one another, and we work together as a team. And I think that's the main thing. If you've got good work colleagues, that makes a world of difference.

I worked through Covid-19. It was quite a frightening thing because no one knew anything about it. All you heard was what was on the news, and then all of a sudden, out of the blue, our ward became a Covid ward overnight, totally unexpected. The manager came up to me and another domestic on the ward and said, 'Girls, could you do me a favour? This ward will become a Covid ward tomorrow and the place is going to need a quick clean around, would you be able to do that?' At which point me and Jan were absolutely petrified. But we went and cleaned around, tidied as best we could.

There were three wards combined together to make the Covid ward. I think that's about 70-odd beds in total. It was frightening. My main thought was I've got a husband at home who has a low immune system, and I was worried about taking it home to him. But if everyone turned around and said, 'Oh, I don't want to do that,' there'd be no one left working on the ward.

So in the end, I just did it. I just worked. I went home every night to my husband. When we came onto the ward, we came in our own uniform or our own clothes, then we had to go and change into scrubs. We were all wearing scrubs: doctors, nurses, everyone was in scrubs, so there was a lot of confusion. Quite often people came up to me saying, 'Oh nurse, can you do this,' and I would have to turn around and say, 'Oh, I'm sorry, I'm not a nurse, I'm just a domestic.' Once a doctor turned round and said, 'Don't say you're *just* a domestic, you're just as important.' That meant a lot to me.

One time, I had my scrubs and masks on and a doctor came to talk to me about a patient. He thought I was another doctor and I had to turn around and say, 'I'm a domestic!' and he said, 'We all look alike now, don't we?'

10

Once we were on the ward, we had to stay on the ward. To leave, I had to get changed, and then when I came back onto the ward, I had to get changed and get scrubbed up again. Rather than do that each time, it was a lot easier just to stay. Sometimes I'd be there for ten hours a day and not go off. I'd' just eat my lunch there. On a normal day, I'd go and get my meal somewhere – maybe pop to the shop or go and sit in the restaurant and mingle with other people, but during Covid, once I was there, I stayed. During Covid, a lot of companies were sending food onto the ward, which I thought was really nice.

We had a 'wobble room' – basically it's just a room where if you get a bit upset or you need someone to talk to, or you just want a bit of time to yourself, you can go and sit in there. I've made use of that room many, many times.

I'd never really experienced death in all my thirteen, fourteen years of working at the hospital, apart from the odd occasion. It was not a regular thing. But during Covid, it obviously became more frequent. It did upset me because I've never seen it on that scale. People would come in – the majority of them elderly people – and you knew that once they came in, they weren't leaving, and I did find that distressing. They weren't allowed visitors, so for a lot of the patients that came onto the ward, that was it. That was the last time they would see their family. Their last minutes would be alone and frightened in hospital, if we didn't have people like Monica sitting with them.

During lockdown, when I came home from work, as soon as I walked through the door, I basically had a tub of gel next to the door as soon as I walked in. I gelled my hands, took all my clothes off and ran straight upstairs and had a bath before I came anywhere near my husband. I didn't want to bring anything back from the hospital to him. I think I probably did give it to him because I caught Covid within a month of our ward becoming a Covid ward. I caught it along with a load of other staff on the ward.

I think the NHS is very, very important, and I think we're lucky to have it. So many people in other countries can't afford healthcare. If you get ill, that's it really, you have to pay for everything, and some people can't afford it, they can't afford medication. So in this country, I think we're really lucky to have that because there are so many people that need it. If we lost it, that would be a shame.

I've seen many changes over the years. The nurse's home, which is now gone. The loss of the children's ward and A&E. I remember having my son here in 1989 when we used to have a maternity unit which has now gone. I still love it here because the people are friendly, and I'm proud to work here. This hospital was visited by Aneurin Bevan, the health minister of the time in 1948 when it was known as Park Hospital. This is where the NHS started, the birthplace of the NHS.

This is What I Say

Gillian Lambert

Volunteer

WE ARE A TEAM.
There is someone to help you.
Nothing to fear.
A hard task, but I believe you can do it.
Choose someone to work with you if you like.

Now it's your turn.
You're going to smash this.
The change is in front of you – a big mixed pile.
Perhaps spread it out?
Brilliant.

Now we can start!
I'd like you to find me 89p.
That's tricky, but we'll all be with you.
Perhaps start with 50p – it's big, silver and has lots of sides.
You've got it – great.

Now find 20p – it's small, silver and has lots of sides.
Good – pop them to one side together so we don't get muddled.

To find how much we've got all together – forget the zeros for a
  sec and count on an extra 2 after 5.
5,6,7 and put the zero back, making 70p.

Now another round silver coin – not the tiny one, we need that
  in a minute.
Yes, 10p, making 80p.

You're nearly there!
Now the tiny silver coin. Can anyone help by adding 5 to 80?
Smashing – 85p

There are only 2 more to find and that's easier as they're both the
  same!
Brown and round.
The bigger of the coins.
Two that match.

2p + 2p equals?
Excellent 85p + 4p = 89p!

You've done it!
You're a winner!

Why Trafford?

Michelle Davies

Librarian

AFTER MOVING NORTH FROM London for the sake of love, I started
working for Central Manchester Trust in 2004, as the librarian for
Pendlebury and Blackley Children's Hospital libraries. I'd tried
several different library settings but chose to be a librarian in a
hospital as I wanted to contribute to something that was such a
key part of society. An institution that has helped my family and
friends in multiple moments of mind and body weakness.

A hospital is a community within itself, where a myriad of
professions and staff find connections and all contribute to the
same cause: one of the basics of life, healthcare. We're all working
to find the best fit, evidence-based answers for overall practice
and individual cases. Providing access to information sources,
books, and assisting staff with queries and training allows me to
have my own corner in this set up – metaphorically in the
structure and literally in a shared-space library! A service for
every member of staff whether learning, studying, researching, or
needing guidance and time out for well-being and escapism.

We merged all of the hospital libraries into one facility from
2007–2009, based on the Oxford Road campus alongside the
newly sited hospitals as part of a Private Finance Initiative build.
Hard work and a great change for us all, but as it had been the

plan since the day I started, I mostly felt prepared for this. The addition of Trafford to the Trust happened while I was on maternity leave in 2012, and on my return to work, I was keen to go over to meet my new colleagues. For the first six months I took the internal bus from Oxford Road to Trafford once a week, and due to a propensity for travel sickness, often arrived headachy and weak, or dreading the return journey back! I persevered though, and Helen the librarian always offered to make me a drink when I walked in as a much-needed distraction. And that's how Trafford Hospital has always felt to me – don't worry now that you're here, we'll help each other. The Trust has since further expanded, with each site spread across Manchester, all having their own local feel. What's always struck me about the Trafford site though, was the trees. Although mostly surrounded by a residential area, it instantly felt like a very green site. When I learnt to drive, the first non-family passenger in my car was Elaine from the library to help me navigate the correct onsite parking – as I drove down the main road at the front of the building I nearly turned in on the wrong side of the entrance as I distracted myself marvelling at the welcoming setting! Over the years, and with library staff changes, my involvement with Trafford has changed, but I'm now proud to be associated with the historical first NHS hospital. Each working day includes trips to the restaurant, security, cashiers, the post room, the WRVS all with friendly corridor waves, hellos, and conversations along the way. We all go off to our separate wards, offices, and rooms, but the clock tower allows us to navigate around the site surrounding it, and the blue plaque a reminder of the fabulous history and achievements that we can all take pride in.

Covid Diary

Martha Sheen

Nurse

Shift 1 of 21 – First positive Covid-19 patient. Intense. Had multiple previous contacts. Unsure how this is going to pan out. Nando's brought in free chicken and Leoncino brought in pizza. Survived the shift. Started self-isolating in my room.

Shift 2 of 21 – Two query Covid-19 patients. Positive Covid-19 patient moved to another ward. Free items from the Body Shop, much needed, hands are insanely dry. Nice shift.

Shift 3 of 21 – Four query Covid-19 patients. Average shift. Grandpa spent the night in hospital. Awaiting tests.

Shift 4 of 21 – The UK went into lockdown. Worked on another ward today. Two bays of query Covid-19 patients. Staff on ward very anxious. Grandpa diagnosed with metastatic bladder cancer (spine, bladder, lung). Free Krispy Kreme donuts and flowers from M&S. Phoned Grandma to discuss current situation with Grandpa.

Shift 5 of 21 – Worked on another ward, theatres shut, staff helping on wards. Four query Covid-19 patients. Quite stressful shift.

Shift 6 of 21 – Two query Covid-19 patients, two positive patients on ward, partner of another patient. More Krispy Kreme donuts. Relatively calm shift.

Shift 7 of 21 – Worked on another ward, early shift, staff insanely anxious. Late shift. Another positive patient. Briefly worked on another ward. Everyone clapped the NHS at 8pm. Very emotional. Family did it again for me coming home. Shift 7 of 21, think I'm coping well.

Shift 8 of 21 – Relatively quiet and settled. D and I made well-being bags for colleagues, everyone really appreciated it. Big companies donated large amounts of 'goodies', got some pretty nice, cute bits. Spent most of my shift on another ward. Very busy, no staff.

Shift 9 of 21 – Working on same ward. N got moved, very busy morning. Two patients passed away. Very sad times due to new visiting restrictions. Did 5k which was very good for my mental health. Family quiz and free Deccan curry.

Shift 10 of 21 – Moved to another ward today. Busy but nice shift. Did online quiz with friends. Nice day.

Shift 11 of 21 – Moved to another ward today. Clearing out ward for any positive Covid-19 patients. Spoke to Grandpa on the phone. Perfect end to a crazy day.

Shift 12 of 21 – Quiet. All positive Covid-19 patients to be moved to another ward. Total of five positive patients with multiple query positives.

Shift 13 of 21 – Weird shift, everyone very stressed. This ward to be made into Covid ward. Intense. The beginning of the storm.

Shift 14 of 21 – Cleared all Covid-19 positive patients to one ward, cleared and cleaned another ward. Started admitting from another MFT hospital, very busy shift.

Shift 15 of 21 – Did long day instead of early, took patient to Covid ward, very busy shift.

Shift 16 of 21 – Fairly busy, finished two hours late. Did family quiz, had very nice catch-up with them all. Rang Grandma (daily basis now), Grandpa to be moved to hospice.

Shift 17 of 21 – Late shift today. Went to another ward first for patient's 91st birthday, cake and card from staff. Had a cry with a colleague and a patient. Struggling now, cried for solid hour, spoke to Grandma. Not sure how much more of this I can take. Grandpa to be moved to hospice. Had our first Covid death at Trafford. Sad ending that shouldn't have happened.

Shift 18 of 21 – Slept terribly, never a good start. Relatively calm shift. Spoke to Grandpa on the phone. He really is the best human.

Shift 19 of 21 – Very busy, mainly due to mad increase in staff. Alright shift, got some free KFC, spoke to Grandma on the phone.

Shift 20 of 21 – Long day on the ward, very busy. Slowly getting sorted, the days are getting harder, all Covid-19 positive or query Covid-19. Relatives still not allowed to visit, making it even harder.

Shift 21 of 21 – Busy, tough day. Death two overnight, male patient on end-of-life care, wife came to visit to say goodbye. My heart is breaking for all these poor patients and their families on a daily basis, more than ready for a day off and a large gin.

/

Day off – Finally a day off. Grandpa diagnosed with Covid-19. My heart is struggling to cope and I can't take much more. Relaxed in garden, had some gins and a couple laughs with the S's. Going to need some serious TLC post-pandemic.

/

Shift 1 of 7 – Late shift. Very busy. Three more deaths taking the total to five. Finished work late, Sundays are always the longest and hardest. Grandpa passed away late evening. My heart has never been so heavy.

Shift 2 of 7 – Tough day barely slept. Got up for early shift, pretty busy, getting better. Phoned Grandma, going to be a difficult few weeks. Did some fitness for the first time in a while.

Shift 3 of 7 – Early shift. Death six, very sad. The girls (and general good people in my life) dropped off a basket of 'essential items'. I'm very lucky to have people like this around me. Facetime session with friends. Happy birthday Grandpa, you were one of the best.

Shift 4 of 7 – Early shift. Two more deaths overnight (eight in total) becoming a daily struggle. A patient's (T) family (known since I started at Trafford) phoned to say goodbye to T, very sad shift. Had catch-up with friends, discussed ongoing situation. Phoned Grandma. Sorted well-being bags.

Shift 5 of 7 – Early shift. Patient from yesterday passed away overnight (Covid-19). Nice shift, early finish to give out well-being bags, hopefully improve morale on the ward, it's getting very difficult.

Shift 6 of 7 – Long day, busy busy. Patient who didn't seem very poorly passed away early hours (M) plus two other patients, one that Mum knew, total to twelve. Many patients gone to other wards and a couple have gone home – it's not all bad, felt a little sad hearing about Mum's friend. Phoned Grandma. She was a little bit sad, we discussed our upcoming holiday to Scarborough.

Shift 7 of 7 – Early shift. Average level of busy. Married couple in side room, husband very poorly, end-of-life care, distressing for wife. Had a bath and a gin, going to learn the piano (again). Phoned Grandma.

/

Day off – Had a lie-in until 10.30am (rare for me). Got a text about working today or tomorrow, opted for tomorrow. Had a beer in the sun, pasta for tea. Returned to my room. Phoned Grandma and family quiz.

/

Shift 1 of 3 – Early shift. Busy. Ended up agreeing to stay until 8pm. Three patients passed away overnight (fifteen total). Husband passed away, very distressing for wife. Long busy shift. Phoned Grandma.

Shift 2 of 3 – Long day. Busy shift. Nice team which helps. Everyone is getting rather stressed. Patient passed away early evening, FaceTimed his daughter earlier that day. Phoned Grandma. Backache.

Shift 3 of 3 – Long day on Ward 12. Rather good shift for the first half, second half was very busy. Patient went off and quite poorly. Two patients on end-of-life care. Struggling and tired.

Back aches. Phoned Grandma. Relaxed in bed before going to sleep.

/

Day off – Hardest day of my life, Grandpa's funeral. Stopped off at Grandma's, she said her goodbyes. I had to wear a facemask, the service was twenty minutes, seated two metres apart and no eulogy. Tough day. Had a curry in the garden with many a gin and tonic.

/

Shift 1 of 14 – Slept badly. Patient had passed away upon arrival to work. Son was present. Assisted with laying out – always sad. Work let me finish at 5pm instead of 8pm. Struggling a bit and feeling very depressed. Sat with Dad in the garden while family took hamper of shopping to Grandma. Had a really nice chat with Dad. Bed.

Shift 2 of 14 – Long day. Good team on the ward. Couple of poorly patients. A few relatives came in. A busy start and busy end to the shift. Home. Phoned Grandma. Bed.

Shift 3 of 14 – Early shift. Patient death overnight, relatives visited yesterday and a couple days previous. Finished around 4ish. Phoned Grandma on walk home. Did a 5k after work with G, really enjoyed it. Had a gin and tonic in the garden and relaxed. Relatively good, productive day.

Shift 4 of 14 – Early shift. M passed away overnight, spent a lot of time with her on the ward. Total to nineteen. Spent a fair bit of time today sorting out paperwork. Finished early, gave a well-being bag to a colleague. Home. Phoned Grandma, lovely as always. Did a 5k and sorted 2019 scrapbook. Very therapeutic and nice to look back. Relaxed and bed.

Shift 5 of 14 – Started shift on ward – patient got discharged. Patient number five! Good start to the shift. Stayed on this ward until about 1.30 then reopened another ward, busy but doable. Expecting sixteen patients but only got five. One very poorly (M) who has been in previously. Wife came in to see him. Another patient transferred to Covid ward as query Covid positive. Very stressful for family. Phoned Grandma.

Shift 6 of 14 – Long day shift. Relatively settled morning. M's wife spent some time on the ward after visiting M, very poorly. I was moved to another ward for the late shift. Very busy. Phoned Grandma. Really missing her.

Shift 7 of 14 – Early shift, ended up getting moved to another ward. Very busy but survived. Patients requiring lots of support. Phoned Grandma. Did a 5k. Clapped for carers, very busy was very heart-warming.

Shift 8 of 14 – Long day. Was on one ward for the day, and then moved to another ward for the late shift. P told me I'm wanted at Trafford General Hospital clock tower on Thursday for the clap (sounds interesting). Tried to sort ward out on late shift. Stayed with patient (J) as he was major agitated.

Shift 9 of 14 – Long day. Busy shift but alright on the whole. I am starting to get very tired of all of this. Missing my family and friends a lot. Emotional struggle. Phoned Grandma.

Shift 10 of 14 – Early shift. Busy shift, a couple of poorly patients. Starting to reswab patients and a few are coming back negative which is great news. Five patients so far have been directly discharged home which is wonderful. 25-30 deaths on this ward due to Covid 19 which is insanely hard going. Hoping this is the beginning of the end. Phoned Grandma which always cheers me up.

Shift 11 of 14 – Early shift. Busy but nice shift, enjoy dementia care. Saw J (patient with wife O) who is much better, had negative Covid-19 swab and waiting to go home and be with O. Did 5k with G, nice finish to a nice day. Phoned Grandma and did a quiz with the girls.

Shift 12 of 14 – Early shift today, but improving on there for sure. Our patient R was discharged (patient who has been in hospital since December 2019) after recovering from a fall, four bouts of illness and covid. I couldn't be happier for R and his family. Came home, started 5k with G but he got a call out at around 2k, so came home, had tea in the garden. Phoned Grandma.

Shift 13 of 14 – Early shift today, busy but getting generally better. The ward I used to work on seems to be getting busier so will hopefully be back there next week. Did a 5k run with G, nice weather. Phoned Grandma.

Shift 14 of 14 – Early shift, very busy shift, didn't stop. Sorted some ward stuff on another ward and got things ready for F's birthday on Saturday. Nipped home (briefly), went back to Trafford General to clap for carers at 8pm, was very overwhelming to see the police, fire service, paramedics and other NHS (MFT) workers. Honoured to have been asked, really enjoyed it. Phoned Grandma.

First Day at Work

Amanda Jordan

Radio Station Manager & HR

I DRIVE INTO TRAFFORD General car park with a sense of excitement and nerves. It is a mild, sunny day and I easily find a parking space to leave my yellow jalopy and head to my new office. I didn't know it then, but it would be my home for the next ten years. Ten happy, fun, and sometimes sad and challenging years.

I walk to the dilapidated modular building that reminds me somewhat of a cow shed! Take a breath and head in. Time to start my first real HR job in the NHS.

The corridor smells musty. It's dark but warm. I see a friendly, inquisitive face peering from the glass window at the end of the dimly lit corridor. 'Hello, you must be the newbie,' she says. She shows me around and I meet my new colleagues. They are welcoming and friendly. My nerves start to subside.

My new line manager initiates me into the ways of the NHS before adding, 'We're a bit short-staffed.' On that first day, he also told me, 'Don't worry if you get something wrong, it can always be fixed.' This made me feel safe and supported and is a mantra and wisdom I have taken with me on my own journey as a manager.

The sense of community and family in my time at Trafford is one I will never forget. I was born here, I live here, I am a patient here, I worked here and I volunteer here. It is home.

The Porters

Kim Moore

Writer-in-Residence

WE MOVE ANYTHING THAT needs moving
furniture oxygen nitrous gases
we empty the bins or take the post

we deliver the drugs the bloods
the patients
from one side of the hospital to another

the dead bodies
from this world to the other
once we were taxi drivers

welders printers bar staff
now we're here
we walk ten miles a day

or twelve miles a day
down long corridors
flights of stairs

we say Mavis *what you like on your feet*
she replies *I like my socks*
and slippers thanks

can you imagine that
90 years old and mind
still quick as a flash

remember that porter
who hid in the fridge
remember when he hid

inside the hatch
how did he get in there
and out again

no we can't tell you
about the jokes
they wouldn't be funny

written down
during covid we worked
double shifts

postman and porter
no it never crossed
our minds not to go

to work
it felt like war
it felt like duty

we slept in separate bedrooms
from our wives
to keep them safe

or in caravans on the drive
we did that ourselves
nobody really told us to

we didn't know
what we were up against
and when the PPE ran out

we scavenged for more
for gloves
all whilst moving anything

that needed moving
the patients yes
in wheelchairs or beds

but also the drugs
the bloods the bins
the post the desks

and tables and yes
of course the bodies
yes of course the dead

For Steve S, Steve J, Warren, Charlie, Jed and Reece

Shine like a Diamond

Monica Donnelly

Nursing Assistant

I WORK AT TRAFFORD General Hospital in Ward 12 as a nursing assistant. I've been working here for the last six years. I always wear my badges to work – they say that I'm a diamond! I won the Diamond Award for NHSP (National Health Service Professionals) and a Diamond Award for looking after the environment. I'm really proud of my badges.

I came to the UK from Jamaica in 1998. I was working with a charity over there, and they had a raffle. When they picked my number out, my prize was a trip to the UK! It was my first time travelling and I met this lady, and I went to have a facial in her salon – and that's where I met my husband. I had a facial mask on and he said, 'Oh, what a lovely lady!', and you know, the rest is history.

I had to go back to Jamaica, but guess what, he came after me, and we got married in Jamaica, got all our paperwork in order and then I migrated to England in 2008. It was a very lucky raffle ticket!

Before I came to England, I used to look after my grandmother, and everyone always said, 'Monica, you need to be a nurse.' So when I came and started working at the care home, and then they closed, I went to another care home. I said to them, 'I'm not really going to stay, I'm just waiting to hear from the NHS.' And everyone was crying because they knew I loved my job, and I always put my patient first. People think I'm the manager, even though I don't get the salary, but I make sure everyone feels at home. Sometimes people come for surgery and a patient might get very anxious, and my manager says, 'Can you follow the patient to surgery and calm them down.' She says I have a knack for it.

I say, 'OK, my name is Monica, and I'll be looking after you today.' Sometimes a patient might start crying. And I say, 'Listen, I'm here. If you need anything, squeeze my hand, I'll be here for you. I know you're an independent person, but when you come into hospital, you have to give up a bit of that independence. It will only be for a couple of days.' Afterwards, I say, 'Come on now, your surgery is done.' And they might have surgery on their knees, or the hip – and they might be worried that they can't turn. And I say, 'Yes, you can turn on that hip.' When they go home, they always write to us and say, 'Oh my God, Monica put me at ease.' I try to be there and try and calm any situation. Sometimes I start singing, and they say, 'Oh! I didn't know you can sing!' I just love to sing.

You always have to put patient care in front. We don't do it for the money – we want the patients to come in, get the surgery and get them on the road to recovery. They know we are there for them. Sometimes they might get upset or frustrated, but afterwards they often apologise. I say, 'Listen. There's no problem.' Later they ring the manager or write a letter saying thank you.

When we ask patients what matters to them, they say, 'A smiling nurse, management of pain and going home,' and that's what we try and do at Trafford.

Coming from the Caribbean, I think the NHS is amazing. It's not just for the rich, it's for everyone. If we didn't have the

NHS, I don't know how people would manage the pain. We cannot take the NHS for granted – it does a world of good for everyone.

My mom and dad lived in Kingston, so I lived with my grandmother. Jamaica exports bananas to England so on a Saturday, I would carry my banana to market and then they would sell it and send it to England, and I got a little pocket money. I was about ten years old then. So my work ethic has always been, you have to work for what you want. I always say, 'Do not grudge a person for what they have, because you don't know how they come by it.' And I always live by that motto. If you do good, good will follow you.

During Covid, we didn't know what we were doing at first because it was something new, but yet we got through it. My manager asked me to go and sit with a patient, and I went and sat with that patient until he took his last breath. That's our job.

We had to make sure that person was comfortable at the end of their life, make everything peaceful and that they have dignity, because, without dignity, there's nothing.

My ward became a Covid ward. And I was there 24/7, and I give thanks I did not catch Covid that whole time. But one day I would come in and see a patient, the next day you come in and they're not there. We had a wife and a husband and both of them died.

But because we have the strength and we have our managers and the staff behind us, we would just rally and do our job.

We would come into hospital in our street clothes, then we would change into scrubs. We had a quiet room, so when things got too hectic for us, we could go in there, sit and explain things and start again.

When we had patients that got over Covid and got to go home, we lined up and clapped them as they left. We were so happy to see them go home.

Listen, I'll go on the mountain and sing for the NHS and sing for my job because I love it.

I do feel as if I've processed all of it now. We have people we can talk to; we don't just have to bottle it up. We just worked as a team, and if you have a good team, anything is possible.

The Stethoscope

Anjali Santhakumar

Consultant

My old faithful stethoscope,
abandoned in the back seat of my car.
Once a lovely vibrant shade of blue I had chosen with delight –
now forlorn in an awful shade of red –
close to blood.

For years I trod purposefully
carrying this obnoxious thing.
A valuable tool working perfectly.
Ignoring for a long time
this frightful sight to behold.

The curious colleagues have asked me
and the polite patients have ignored it.
It is the polite ones,
the quiet ones
I wonder about.

Do they think I am a glorious warrior,
fighting Covid battles shedding blood, sweat and tears?
A true claimant to the uneasy hero cape we all wore?
My faithful 'bloody' stethoscope

a badge of honour?
I try to hold onto this glorious image in vain
But no,
they probably just think I am gross!
To the curious people who have asked me
Eeks... is that blood?

I answer 'No! It's crayons my children have had fun with
A perfectly reasonable answer
to people with kids.
To my closest confidante I spill the secret, alas!
It was a run-in with an open lipstick in my bag.

I can ignore this ugly thing
around my neck no longer.
Sadly, my once perfect
faithful stethoscope now lies
disused and unloved.

Around my neck
lies a new stethoscope
in a fetching shade of purple.
Perhaps a new weapon
for battles unknown.

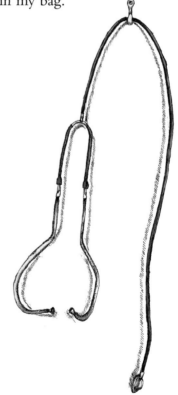

Who You Gonna Call

Thomas Lee

Domestic Assistant

I'VE BEEN WORKING AT Trafford for nearly sixteen years now, from 2007. My job title is a domestic assistant, working through Facilities. Part of my job is to clean wards, departments, public areas and so on – public toilets, that sort of thing. I go around, and I clean every single carpet you see and each bay in the ward.

I'm mostly on public areas, but my supervisors call me or find me in the morning if they need to put me anywhere else. If they need me to do anything else, I'm quite happy to do it. I interact with patients and visitors – they often ask me to get them where they need to go, so I point them in the right direction. When I'm working on wards, the patients ask me things like do I enjoy working here and stuff like that. They always ask me that!

My grandma used to work at Trafford as well – she worked with the porters – she was a Porter Supervisor. I think it was the 1970s she started, and then she retired in 2014. I worked here for seven years whilst my grandmother was still here. She always checked in on me to see if I was getting on alright, and if I was getting into it – I would always say, 'Yes, I'm getting into it!' She trained me up on a few things, like we had these floor polishers we used to use – I don't use them anymore because someone else does that job.

I've got this Hoover which sits on your back, you have to strap it, and it's got all these back supports and stuff. The Hoover can be very heavy, if you've not got it on properly, it does hurt your back. It hurt mine a bit last week because I was trying to get it on and it was all twisted, so I had to sort all of that out. This Hoover is corridor use only because you can't use normal hoovers because they have cords, and you can't have cords in a corridor because it's a trip hazard. Even though you've got wet signs across the corridor, people still ignore them and end up falling over. Anyway, the Hoover is really heavy, but once you've got it on properly with all the back supports it's not a problem. Every time I'm going around the corridor with it, people say, 'You look like a ghostbuster with it,' – so I stuck loads of ghostbuster stickers on the back of it, and they all seem to love it. It's like a ghostbuster's proton pack – they are square, mine is cylinder. Nobody else uses this particular Hoover.

Today I'm cleaning in pre-op – today and tomorrow, because I'm covering for someone, and the pre-op staff love it when I'm walking through. They always say to me, 'Ey up, Tom's here with his ghostbuster.' They just love it; it makes their day.

They always say to me 'Who you gonna call?' and I say, 'You're gonna call me!'

I've been here a long time. I worked through Covid – it was tough, I just got on with it. I've never had Covid – touch wood, and I don't want it. I've seen what a bad illness it is.

I've had loads of funny moments with staff, and loads of good moments. What's different with the NHS – the rate's good. I've always wanted to work in a hospital – my grandmother was here. And you're doing different things rather than the same thing every day. You're going to different places, you're cleaning different areas – if I was working in a supermarket, I'd just be doing the same thing every time, which is not my sort of thing. I wanted to do a job where I could do different things – where I could work with staff members and as part of a team.

Words of Wisdom

Angela Reeve

Facilities Catering Manager

1. Onions are a gift to the world.

2. To write a poem, look out into the yonder.

3. To be happy, count the pigeons on the solar panels.

4. Or eat Jaffa Cakes and Creme Eggs.

5. Keep an eye on the daffodils.

6. Don't buy reduced ones.

7. Everybody deserves a moment.

8. Loose lips sink ships.

9. I'm never wrong.

10. It's OK to be a basic model.

11. If in doubt, throw it in the skip.

12. If you're gonna try your best, turn up.

Ebb and Flow

Anna Jerram

Vascular Scientist

It was July 2004. A memory inked so vividly, it feels like it happened just yesterday. Passing through the painfully-slow-to-open automatic entrance doors of Manchester Royal Infirmary for the first time; the gateway to what was to be not only a new job, but my career. A tiny, yet integral brushstroke. My small (but not insignificant) mark to make, on the vast, diverse, and colourful canvas of the NHS – then 56 years in the painting.

Following the otherwise featureless, shiny-floored maze of corridors through the hospital, a porter smiled and nodded at me with a look of misplaced recognition. I had served him his hard-earned after-work pint only months before, in my former role as a part-time student bartender at the pub on the corner, which joined the sprawling hospital site to the bustling campus of The University of Manchester. The corner I'd turned just that morning, between my recent past as a struggling and disillusioned biology student, to my imminent future as a trainee vascular scientist.

I had never heard of a vascular scientist before I inadvertently stumbled across an advert in a jobseekers' newspaper; brought home by my partner who conveniently worked in a job centre at the time. It was a moment that felt like fate, but was probably just jolly good timing. I was nearing my final year exams, and the prospect of the void which lay beyond them loomed all too uncomfortably close. My love affair with all things science related – which had blazed hotter than the blue flame of a Bunsen burner throughout my secondary school and college years – had dwindled to a barely glowing ember in the midst of my university experience. I was burnt out and depressed, convinced that I'd fall at the final hurdle, with no inkling of my direction in life for the very first time. Up to that point, everything had seemed so mapped out. Now, I just felt lost.

Something about that job advert spoke to me. I felt strangely excited about something for the first time in a long time. Maybe it was just the slim possibility that the hard slog of a degree I'd fought my way through might finally be for something – a possible passport to my next destination. But it also sounded like a job that might suit me. Or maybe more so, that I might suit it.

I had always felt drawn to a career in healthcare. I'd toyed with the idea of studying medicine for a while, then talked myself out of it at the peak of a teenage confidence crisis. My high school work experience placements had been in a pharmacy and a hospital radiography department, and I had volunteered as a care assistant at a local care home for the elderly and in the Lourdes pilgrimage hospitals.

I knew it was a long shot to apply, possibly bordering on cheeky: I hadn't even got my degree yet. But I had nothing to lose and potentially something substantial to gain. So, I hurriedly filled in the application form and popped it in the post box, before I had time to talk myself out of that, too. Raised in a Catholic church-going family, I found my relationship with faith and religion confused and conflicted throughout my turbulent teenage years. So, it tickled me to find myself praying that I would at least get an interview. As the spoilers above might suggest, my prayers were answered: I did get an interview and, to my disbelief, I was offered the job on the condition that I passed my exams, and my degree was in the bag. And that was just the push I needed to get across the finish line. I got my degree, somehow, and the next chapter of my journey was about to begin.

Tentatively pushing open the door marked 'Vascular Laboratory', I was unknowingly stepping into the department in which I was to spend the best part of my working life, eventually splitting my time between Manchester Royal Infirmary and Trafford General Hospital. A tidal wave of imposter syndrome crashed over me, just like it had on my first day of primary school. Mum's comical recollection of my meltdown that morning, when I proclaimed that I couldn't possibly go in because I couldn't read, couldn't write, and couldn't play netball, was suddenly in full re-enactment beneath my deceptively calm exterior. Thankfully by this point, I could read *and* write (netball skills remained dubious), but I didn't have the foggiest idea about how to do a vascular ultrasound scan.

Flashbacks of the faulty flicker from an old X-ray lightbox on the wall. Long-sleeved, trailing, unhygienic white lab coats, long since outlawed by hospital infection control policy. The steady, rhythmic beat of a patient's pulse drumming through the door of a nearby clinic room. All irrevocably etched on my anxious whirring, stirring mind that first day. The first of many days, which came and went in a flurry of unfamiliar faces, places, skills, and concepts to quickly learn and remember.

As I apprehensively opened the textbooks to get better acquainted with this new-fangled field, tongue-twisting terminology came at me thick and fast: the foreign dialect of vascular science and surgery. And quite unexpectedly, somewhere in the learning of this new language; along the path to making vascular feel vernacular, I felt fuel on that dying fire. A reignition of my interest in science, and the confidence to study again, sparked at the coalface of a healthcare profession which felt vocational.

Sights and smells I had never imagined possible would now be encountered daily, as I progressed through the training program to perform and perfect the art of the vascular ultrasound scan. Sick bowls and stoma bags; leg ulcers and gangrene. Blackened, bloated, oxygen-starved toes; the result of a blood supply so narrowed and blocked, it was beyond the point of repair with the plumbing attempts of even the best vascular surgeon. With a stench so extreme you could taste it: the acerbic smack of putrefying flesh. I was taught the trick of a subtle slick of vapour rub, dabbed in the groove between the nose and mouth: a welcome remedy to this repugnant fug (which enabled the illusion of unfaltering professionalism) – its acrid top notes mellowed by the menthol. My childish aversion to this overwhelming olfactory assault would be quickly quashed, however, by the dawning realisation that this poor patient was suffering silently in a world of pain so agonising, any brief discomfort of mine was squished to a scant speck on the distant horizon.

The heartbreaking, humbling experience of working each and every day with people in pain had a profound effect on me. It was a jolt into gaining some perspective on my own worries and problems, and awakened me to the harsh home truth that I still had a fair bit of growing up to do. In my last job, the worst-case scenario was that I served an unsatisfactory pint to a disgruntled customer. Now, the diagnostic test results I reported would signpost the course of a patient's treatment, potentially leading to major surgery or lifelong medication with some serious side effects. It would take me a while to acclimatise to this new level of instilled trust and responsibility. There were times when I wobbled and doubted my ability to see the course through to completion. But I persevered, and in 2007 I passed my postgraduate exams to become an accredited vascular scientist.

The learning never really ends though, in a workplace where

every patient presents with a different lesson to teach you. From seldom seen pathology to bamboozle the brain of even the most experienced practitioner, to a tale of triumph over seemingly impossible adversity which enkindles a new way to look at life. Patients from all backgrounds who had survived earth-shattering episodes: cancer diagnoses, blood clots, heart attacks, strokes and organ failure to name but a few. People who were quite literally facing the prospect of the loss of life or limb, despite the best efforts of the medics and surgeons to salvage both. Perhaps the most inspiring of all were the patients who did indeed lose a limb, but were still living a life, after months of arduous amputee rehabilitation.

Nineteen years on – almost half my lifetime – and I'm still learning. Perhaps the most elaborate lesson of recent years was how to make it through the days that came under the dark dictatorship of Covid-19. The memory of those first months still has a dream-like quality. Hospital corridors once alive with human traffic, were eery and echoing. Haunted by the ghosts of porters pushing patients in wheelchairs and beds, back-and-forth between appointments and departments, staff hurrying and scurrying to clinics and consultations; friends and families stopping to ask for directions, on the way to visit their loved ones.

By that point in my career, I felt I could tackle most situations quite well under pressure. I'd learnt not to sweat the small stuff. But working on the Covid wards during that pre-vaccine period was a whole different ball game. It felt big, and I *was* sweating, profusely. Wrapped head-to-toe in plastic PPE in that sweltering, machine-crammed corral, trying to interpret a diagnostic ultrasound through the fog of a steamed-up safety visor. Convinced that the edges of my well-fitting mask were warping; welcoming unwanted, invisible, airborne invaders into the stream of my stifled, shallow breath. And I had it easy. At least I got to leave the ward once my job there was done; free to breathe more easily out on the cool, deserted corridor and return safely back to base. How the staff confined to the care of the patients on those wards endured those dreadful, demoralising days; my mind still boggles.

Post-pandemic, and the deluge of destruction this virus brought to pass continues to ripple through the undercurrents of daily life in the NHS, as it approaches its 75th year. The undying devastation of lives lost; the melancholy memento of long Covid, still loitering by those unlucky enough to be lumbered with it. Cancelled appointments, procedures and delayed life-changing treatments; the consequences of which are still unfolding.

In the years since I started as a flustered, fledgling trainee, there have been many changes. Colleagues have come and gone; some moving on to pastures new. Others stayed, as assuring and supportive as they were on that first day. Patients came and went too, most returning home after fighting their way to a full recovery. Others sadly lost their battle.

The entrance doors of the hospital still don't open fast enough, and the X-ray box still flickers on the wall above the desk. Otherwise, the hospital site as I knew it in those early days has transformed almost beyond recognition; restructured, merged and developed to meet the ever-increasing demands of a growing and ageing patient population.

As for me, I find that I don't rely on the vapour rub trick quite as much to do my job anymore – nose hairs and tastebuds desensitised by countless gruesome gangrene exposures. Thankfully, the heart-felt emotions which invariably arise for the patients I'm entrusted with the honour of caring for, remain yet to be hardened.

The Moral Battle of HR

Amanda Jordan

Radio Station Manager & HR

I fight back my disdain.
The horror of the act.
I want to escape, be far away,
not have to listen to what they have to say.
But I stay.

I push my feelings.
I extend my hand.
A shadow person stands before me
secreting hurt, distress, pain.
Empathy flows despite myself

I listen without judgement.
I advise without bias.
I present truth, painful but real.

Afterwards, I sit with my solitude for what feels like an age.
I reflect on the battle of ethics against values
Morals against humanity.
I am HR but I am also human.

The Nightingale Hospital

Asma Ahmed

Library Assistant

THINKING BACK TO MY time at the Nightingale Hospital, I felt quite nervous in my first few days, thinking what can I do to help, how can I help with the skills I have. The building felt so vast, but it reminded me of a story told to me by my lovely neighbour Malcolm, who sadly passed away from Covid. Malcolm's father worked at the G–MEX when it was a railway station, and apparently once they had to coax down a monkey that had escaped from somewhere. It still makes me smile when I think of Malcolm telling me that story. He was like a grandad to me, and the whole neighbourhood.

When we were at the Nightingale, it felt as if we were in a bubble, as when you went into the city centre every day it was so quiet. I remember wondering whether I would ever see it thriving again.

We had a room called the 'wobble room' which says it in the name really. We could use that room just to have time to ourselves as it was such a pressurised environment to be working in and sometimes felt overwhelming so if you needed a moment, you could use that room. I just remember this huge chair and just curled up in there and closed my eyes.

I often bump into my colleagues from Nightingale around Manchester Foundation Trust hospitals, and it feels like we have this shared understanding of what it felt like to be there. We shared this unique time of uncertainty, but of being together.

A Small Part in a Big Machine

Elaine Brogan

Library Assistant

I ONLY STARTED WORKING for the NHS in January 2023 at Trafford General Hospital in the Education Library. Walking to the main entrance, on my first day, past the clock tower and the blue plaque with the Ukrainian flag flying in front of them, I felt a sense of anticipation and excitement about being part of something extremely important.

Working at Trafford Library is very different as we don't get lots of users on a day-to-day basis but there is still a lot to do. I have a lot of daily tasks to perform such as reminding users by text and email about their overdue books. I supply articles and documents to users and other libraries and work on adding additions to the ambulance service repository. A lot of my day is spent on Open Athens, looking at users' accounts to see whether they are eligible for access.

Before working at Trafford, I spent twelve years working for Manchester public library service and seven working for Manchester University library service. Trafford is unique because it was the first NHS hospital, and there's a particular calmness about it that is hard to describe. It's full of the most amazing people doing a brilliant job every single day – essential and life-saving jobs. I'm not doing any life saving, but I like to think I'm playing my very small part in a big machine.

If I wasn't working in a library, I would be an artist as I do quite a bit of paper art in my spare time, particularly related to mid-century modern. I also have a degree in Landscape Architecture so maybe I would have been one of them!

Christmas at Radio Wishing Well

Gillian Lambert

Volunteer

RADIO WISHING WELL PRESENTERS were going round wards with a trolley loaded with Christmas chocolates. We were singing carols, accompanied by a beardy folk group. With all us old people were three young women doing their Duke of Edinburgh Awards. We had to move from one floor to another. The lift was too small. Two of the girls had the very heavily laden trolley.

I said I would wait and take the lift when it returned.

I was with a young woman in a wheelchair.

Because we had all tried to get in together, her manoeuvring had become difficult, and she was now wedged diagonally in the lift. I am not the strongest person in the world. I had to stick my bum out to prevent the lift doors closing.

We struggled and pushed and pulled and eventually, the young woman shot out like a champagne cork.

Luckily, we were both in fits of giggles – which can be dangerous after a certain age – but all was well, and we awarded ourselves with the label: 'Nicest person to have been stuck in a lift with.'

The Importance of Empathy

Mike Ainsworth

Domestic Assistant

I'VE WORKED AT TRAFFORD for just over a year. For a long, long time I've been wanting to get a job here, but always something happened, or I didn't meet the criteria or whatever. Anyway, eventually I saw a job come up as a Domestic, went for an interview, and the same afternoon, they phoned me up and said you've got the job, so it was happy days! I was quite pleased actually.

I've done a few things before this. A season in Butlins as a barman. My main job when I left school was an engineer. I did about 35 years in engineering – a bit of warehouse work, a bit of delivery driving, a bit of taxi driving – but I always wanted to work at the hospital. It's a good cause job, isn't it, if you know what I mean. Empathy is so important, and the older I've got, the easier I've found it to show that empathy. I think that's partly because I've mellowed from what I used to be like. If you can put a smile on somebody's face, just once, you've had a good day.

Of all the domestics, I'm probably the most public-facing one, because I'm on the corridors all the time. I'll say to somebody, 'Do you know where you're going?' and they'll say, 'Oh, I'm not sure,' and then they show you their letter, and I walk them down, have a chat with them, give them a bit of time out of my day.

I've been very, very lucky, to have the pleasure of working with some of the nicest people. A good 90 per cent of the people who come through the door here professionally say good morning, good afternoon – doctors, nurses, the other domestics – they're all really nice people, which is a surprise, especially when you've worked in factories or warehouses your whole life. I've had some good laughs here, and considering I've only been here a year, I've made some good friends, which is nice. And coming to work now for me – whereas you'd get up in the morning and think, 'Oh god, I've got to go back in there again' – I don't have that now. I don't have that anymore. I actually enjoy my work because the day absolutely flies.

I get up at twenty to four and make a cup of tea. I can't leave the house without a cup of tea, then I get washed, dressed and on my way to work for 5am. I use a machine that I sit on to clean the corridors. It has a couple of brushes and pads which come down, rotate, scrub the floor with cleaning liquid, and then it's got a squeegee on the back with suction which sucks all the dirty water up. I also have to empty the bins on the corridors, make sure the hand sanitisers are all topped up, clean all the ledges, behind the doors, door handles, dusting.

I usually work right through till 9am, and then I have a ten-minute break and work till 12. Then I've got an hour's lunch, and by the time I've had my lunch, I'm packing the machine away, cleaning it down, getting my trolley ready for the next morning. So my day, it really does fly. I've got my own routine, and my own route along the corridors.

My last job was customer services. So I went from factories and warehouses, where every other word is a swear word to somewhere you couldn't swear at all, not a chance. I started work and thought, this is different, but I'm doing alright. Next thing I know my supervisor comes up to me and tells me I've won star of the month. I didn't even know what it was. I asked what for and she said, 'Best customer services advisor for the month. You've won it.' So I carried on in my role and six months later, she came back and she said, 'I hope you don't ever leave, because we've got absolutely nobody on our team who can talk to customers like you can,' and I said 'Well, I'm just me, my normal self!' And she told me that I had this way, this ability, to put them at ease.

Since working here, it's got to the stage where I can see somebody – from a young girl to a young lad, middle-aged man, middle-aged woman, elderly lady, elderly gentleman, and within three seconds of looking at their face, I know how to approach them. Whether it's 'Hello love, how can I help you?' or 'Good afternoon, Madam, can I help?' – I've got this knack, and I don't know where it's come from. I've got no idea whatsoever how I've managed to obtain that ability, but it works. It's a knack – to look at somebody and say – not so much that I know your background, but I know how you want me to speak to you – whether that be formally, informally, jokily – I don't know how I do it. I have absolutely no idea.

I'll be here till I retire now. As I say, this is the first time in my life I can honestly say I don't mind coming to work.

I Remember

Anjali Santhakumar

Consultant

The first time I got paid
for being a real doctor
I bought myself a CD player,
my dad a shirt
and my mum a dress.

The exultation and elation
at passing my exams,
following a truly
fearful moment
before I glanced at the result.

The first patient
who died suddenly –
the sorrow I shared
and the tears I shed
for the family.

The first time I walked
miles across rural India,
across hills and streams

to vaccinate a child
in a remote primary school.

The first time my patient
asked if I'd had a chance
to eat and rest –
the affection and gratitude
I felt towards him.

The brave families
I have talked with
about frailty and loss,
about hope and despair
and all things in between

The first time I put on my PPE
with nothing to offer
but oxygen and words.
And then the last time
with an armful of drugs to help.

The many hospitals and teams
I have worked with
across the UK and India –
the camaraderie and the laughter.
The differences and the likeness.

The Voice

Gillian Lambert

Volunteer

SAM SPOKE TO ALICE all day, every day. He was her reason for getting up in the morning. She knew he didn't live in the radio. That would be silly, but if that's how he chose to communicate with her, fair enough. One day he'd come for her and until then, she'd wait. As long as she could hear his voice.

'It's a safeguarding issue!' Four words from a concerned neighbour would change Alice's life.

The people who came were kind. They had little photos of themselves and clipboards. They asked a lot of questions Alice couldn't answer. Boxes were ticked, files were opened, computers hummed.

Alice couldn't see the looks on their faces once they got back to the car. The smell! The mess! The filth!

Something had to be done.

They came for Alice. She whimpered until they let her put the radio on her lap in the car.

It was a treat to be taken to such a fine house. It was a holiday for Alice. Friendly people helped her. The food was good. She was clean.

And Sam was on the bedside table, talking next to her.

The cleaner was new. It wasn't her fault. She had to plug in the Hoover.

No more Sam.

Alice screamed for seven hours.

No one realised what had happened and she was taken to hospital for tests.

Ayesha was the newest recruit to Radio Hope at the hospital. She wanted to go to Drama School and thought broadcasting would be good experience. But the switches and faders confused her. All the other volunteers seemed to be much older, large men.

This was her second day and Ayesha was nervous. She had been told to go to the wards.

'Set up Hospedia for those who can't! Get requests!'

Ayesha had never been onto a ward. Was she going to see horrors?

Nurses were rushing about, too busy to tell her where to go.

Spotting a little side ward, Ayesha crept in with her Request Slips. There was one patient in a bed. She was moaning softly. Long grey hair. Hardly more than bones under a blanket. Ayesha didn't know what to do. No requests here then. She picked up the bedside Hospedia set and pressed 1. A man's voice announced the next request.

There was silence from the bed. The moaning had stopped. The head moved a little, craning towards the sound. Ayesha adjusted the volume.

Was that a smile? Yes, but a tear as well. Sam was back! He had come for her!

Alice looked into Ayesha's eyes, nodded once, and fell back on the pillow.

Inspired by The Last Quango in Halifax *by Rob Mitchell and Elaine James*

The Laminator Speaks

Michelle Davies

Librarian

I WAS DELIVERED TO the Trafford education centre, bought for the
   library.
My place was next to the printer.
I was next to the golf course, and the nurse's home, looking across
   to the hospital.
Staff and visitors driving past us each day on the busy hospital site.
I laminated simple posters for library staff, students, and clinical
   staff.
about procedures, good practice, opening times, warnings and
   don't forgets.

And then the staff phone calls started over the uncertainty of the
   next day.
And the librarian left suddenly without the planned retirement do.
And the library lights went off and remained off.
I felt the atmosphere of the hospital change.
The door closed and the corridors quietened.
Fewer staff; fewer visitors; nothing to laminate.

One day the door opened: I was taken to Manchester Central –
   distanced security checks on each door.

To an office in a makeshift hospital in what was a train station, turned gig venue, turned conference centre.
To a mixture of staff, a team newly working together, built from multiple departments.
The ongoing questions with no obvious long-term studied evidence to alleviate the puzzled faces of the previously confident and experienced.

How long can the virus live on paper?
Will it help if we laminate posters?
Will the virus live on laminate?
How often should we clean the laminate?
I was needed for new signs to guide – learning and discovering together.
The same forms of communication but new thoughts and vocabulary.
About hand washing, cleaning, decontamination.
Warnings to protect the patients, warnings to protect the staff.

Familiar but new but everchanging – as every hospital always is.
The joke about needing an NHS-dedicated dictionary continuing to be true.
Pandemic – Coronavirus – Covid-19.
Face masks; hot zones; lockdowns; testing; vaccines.

The return to Trafford eventually came.
And I was cleaned down.
And plugged in again for use on everyday posters.
And the staff returned, with new staff and students starting.
And it became familiar again.
But I often think of that time out – a time of change, and how I contributed.

Two Doctors

Anonymous

I WALKED ALONG THE corridor to the relative's room to talk about a 'not for resuscitation' order. I was armed with the golden nugget of information passed on by my nurse that the son was 'medical' and had expressed a wish for his father to remain for resuscitation.

I was going to tell the son that his 87-year-old father had been deemed by the medical team as not suitable to be considered for resuscitation.

I had earlier spoken about resuscitation with the patient – a frail man with a very kind face. He was himself a doctor. He'd listened and quietly agreed that it was for the best. He wanted me to convey this decision to his son.

I went to the small family room on the ward. It had plain white walls and a plainer brown sofa. I had spoken to many families in this room, supporting them through difficult conversations. I'd barely entered the room when the son said abruptly that he wants his father to be resuscitated. He felt unable to agree with the 'not for resuscitation' decision. He pointed out that his dad had been active and was a very accomplished man.

I'd had similar conversations many times, putting across the most pragmatic and persuasive arguments to help family members understand decisions of this nature. I was used to supporting people through difficult discussions around the best interests of a patient. But this time was different.

This time I'd just returned from Greece after burying my 87-year-old dad. My dad had been a distinguished doctor and had earned accolades equivalent to the OBE before being struck down by a heart attack. He had been physically and mentally sharp as ever just before. I'd sat down with his medical team. They proceeded to tell me that resuscitation was not in his best interests.

I had given them all the medical arguments I had and all the reasons why he should be resuscitated. I had refused to even acknowledge the current frailty and state of health of my dad. I'd sat in a big open room with multiple medical team members present. I remember thinking that we'd probably been labelled as a 'difficult family'. They presented me with biochemical evidence of how unwell my father was.

My closest cousin had pointed out to me that 'even the most active person deserves a compassionate death'. I had unwillingly subjugated and with pain laid down all my medical arguments and accepted the decision of the 'not for resuscitation' decision. Forty-eight hours later I had mourned my father's death.

The son sitting across from me now proceeded to give me all the reasons why I should keep his dad to be for resuscitation just as I had with my own father. I outlined all the medical reasons he should not be. I remember the son telling me I spoke very well, but he still wanted his father to be for resuscitation.

I saw myself mirrored in the patient's son; two people fighting for their dads, knowing in their medical heart all the reasons why it would not be in his best interests. Both of us refusing to acknowledge it and fighting hard.

Suddenly I desperately wanted to help this man, more than I ever had before. I wanted to support him to go through and reach as quickly as possible the other end of the painful tunnel I had recently crossed. And so, I began the talk.

For the first time (but not the last), I shared my personal story. After a few moments, he sat back on the brown sofa. His manner changed and a weight seemed to shift.

He paused and asked me what I had done, what decision I had taken. I told him. The conversation afterwards was short. He accepted the decision calmly and was very composed – but I could still see doubts in his eyes. I held his hand in both of mine in an unmoving handshake. Two strangers, two doctors, two sons. And then we parted.

I hope very much that I had in some small way helped him on his journey ahead.

Some details in this story have been changed to protect anonymity.

SEYMOUR
UNIT

Sarah's Story

Anonymous

Support, Time and Recovery Worker

I GREW UP IN the local area, so I knew Trafford General Hospital when I was a child. I can remember visiting a friend's grandma on one of the wards when she was recovering from an illness. I remember we took her some juicy peaches in a brown paper bag. The ward was very long with beds spaced out on either side. When I was a child, it wasn't called Trafford General Hospital but Park Hospital. You still hear people refer to it as Park Hospital today.

Now, many years later, I work on the site of Trafford General Hospital. I work at the Moorside unit, which is a mental health unit. We are run by a separate hospital trust from the main hospital. I work as a support, time and recovery worker on the two later life wards at Moorside. I work doing therapeutic activities with the patients that help to support their recovery. We do activities to help improve patients' mental well-being, for example, art and craft, reminiscence work, quizzes and music. We have regular concerts by Music in Hospitals and Care. These concerts can evoke positive feelings and memories for our patients as they listen to songs from the past from the likes of Frank Sinatra, the Beatles, Tom Jones etc. At the time of writing, I have worked in this post for sixteen years.

I became interested in working in mental health when I was

a patient at the Moorside unit myself in 2002. I was very unwell at the time and would never have thought back then that I could end up working in mental health. However, it just goes to show that recovery is possible. I really enjoy my job and helping people navigate their own recovery journey. It gives you a great feeling to know that you are making a difference to people's lives.

It was when I was a patient at the Moorside unit that I also became a Christian after meeting a fellow patient there who was also a Christian. We got talking and, when she spoke about her Christian faith, it was like a light switched on. Everything made sense. Since then my faith has been a really important part of my life and a source of strength when times are difficult, as they sometimes can be for all of us. I attend a church close to my home; it is also the church where I was christened as a baby.

There have been lots of memorable moments during my working life. However, perhaps the most significant moment was when we heard that the main hospital was on fire.

I vividly remember that summer afternoon in 2021. I had just sat down at the computer to write some patient notes. There was a thunderstorm which seemed to be directly above the hospital itself. I had just picked up a cup of tea and was about to take a sip when I heard an almighty thud of thunder. I nearly jumped out of my skin and, needless to say, my cup of tea went everywhere. I was busy wiping up the spillage when a few minutes later someone came running past the office shouting that the main hospital was on fire. It was the Seymour unit that had caught fire after being hit by lightning.

Fortunately, all the patients and staff were safely evacuated and there were no injuries. The fire brigade worked through the night to dampen down the flames. We really saw the best of humanity that day as staff rallied to help evacuate the patients. A charity even brought a van onto the site and made drinks and snacks for the firefighters to keep their energy levels up. It was a really dramatic event in Trafford General Hospital's history that will no doubt be talked about for years to come.

Little did I think when I was a child visiting Park Hospital that I would end up working there. Hopefully, there are a lot of memorable moments to come, but nothing as dramatic as the fire of summer 2021.

Love You

Martha Sheen

Nurse

ON ONE OF THE days creeping up to my final of 21 shifts, there was an elderly lady admitted who normally lived with her daughter. Both had lost their husbands years ago. They were like best friends. After the mother had been in hospital for four days, the doctors contacted her daughter and told her she was really unwell and might not make it. They gave the daughter the chance to come in but informed her that she had to be in full PPE, and she had to self-isolate for ten days afterwards. She arranged a food delivery and within the hour was by her mother's bedside.

Now, most days when I left the house my dad would wave to me out of his bedroom window and I would shout, 'Bye, love you,' and he'd respond, 'Bye, love you more.' When the daughter had visited her mother, I spoke to her for about fifteen minutes to just reassure her we were going to take great care of her. She told me how much her mum loved Elvis.

As she walked away, she said, 'Goodbye, love. Thank you so much,' and without thinking I shouted, 'Bye, love you,' and we both looked at each other in slight shock. I then very quickly apologised, and she laughed and said, 'It's the first time I've had a "Goodbye, love you" this year and it means a lot.'

Naturally, I then went to the staff room and cried for about ten minutes. Then went and told everyone how I'd just told a patient's relative I loved them. A very ME situation!

The Cardiac Arrest

Anjali Santhakumar

Consultant

'ADULT CARDIAC ARREST IN Ward 24,' crackled the arrest bleep. A once familiar sound, now alien and intrusive, rang out loudly. It was the first day of the industrial strike by the junior doctors and I had volunteered to be part of the cardiac arrest team. I had come into work early, well prepared and wearing my flat comfy trainers – but had I come in with the mental preparedness and expertise I had taken for granted all those years ago…?

I had refreshed my training the previous day and commented that it was like riding a bike; it will all come back to me or… hang on… had someone else told me that?! Regardless it felt true. Questions remained. What role could I assume within the team? I decided I would be a follower rather than a leader today. Doubts if my injury-prone shoulders could cope with the energy and vigour needed for cardiac compressions arose and then were quickly quelled.

One hour to go before the shift ends. This thought had barely crossed my mind when the darned bleep had blared out.

I raced down the long hospital corridor which seemed even longer than I remembered. I ran past a grey-haired lady walking casually along the corridor. She asked me, 'Are you going for the arrest?'

'Yes,' I said as I ran past her. She picked up her pace and joined me and we ran in tandem, striding determinedly, strangers joined together in a common goal. We were nearing Ward 24, a few more metres now and we were ready to save a life. Fuelled with adrenaline, we were ready for a flurry of action when the pager rang out again.

'Cardiac arrest in Ward 24 has been cancelled.'

We stopped in our tracks. A mixture of relief and curiosity flowed through me and I looked at the lady beside me. We said nothing but I saw her emotions mirrored mine. Beaten in our valiant efforts to save a life, we turned back and trudged back together along the same corridor. 'Nice running with you,' I shot out when we parted ways. I returned to my base ward feeling free to audibly pant, now that I was no longer with my composed running partner.

I went back to my ward, returning to smiles from staff who were delighted to see me back so quickly. My unknown patient lives to see another day I thought. I could not help being curious – would our efforts have made a difference to him? For some strange reason, I was certain it was a him! Would me and my shoulders have come through for him? I will never know.

The Visiting Duchess

Jane Gigner-Hollies & Kim Moore

Catering Supervisor

AND THOUGH IT WAS the usual crowd
picked to meet the visiting duchess –
still they wanted to see her, even if
it was just to watch her leaving,

so they slipped out of the walk-in freezers,
through the kitchen and out to the front,
two women still in their overalls
and hairnets, one still chewing gum,

but with immaculate red lipstick
and her hair set because it was Friday,
and the duchess – busy being ushered
into a waiting car – turned around

to say hello. She asked them what
the special was and when they answered 'Fish'
she smiled and said she preferred breaded fish
and they looked at each other and said no,

it's battered today. Battered fish,
and then the duchess laughed
and showed her lipsticked teeth
and let herself be whisked away.

Five Minutes with Jakub Dosa

Jakub Dosa

Facilities Team Leader

KIM: How long have you worked at Trafford?

JAKUB: Five Years

KIM: What does the average day involve in your job?

JAKUB: Ensuring that the patient and visitors receive the service that is expected. For example, safe hot food, clean and safe environment, clean linen, etc.

KIM: Where did you work before you came to Trafford?

JAKUB: I worked for an American restaurant chain for about seven years.

KIM: What are the best/worst bits about the job?

JAKUB: Best: when the service is delivered without any issues. Also, when we see an improvement in the service provision when we implement new ways of working.

KIM: What does the NHS mean to you?

JAKUB: A lot – it's the largest organisation in Europe and I am proud to be working for the NHS.

KIM: What made you want to work in a hospital?

JAKUB: To learn and develop my skills and to experience the public sector.

KIM: Why is Kim so amazing?

JAKUB: Who said that?

KIM: It's like getting blood out of a stone! I am going to make something up. Jakub was once a pirate who made his living as the ship's cook before deciding to hang up his eye patch on the shores of Manchester.

JAKUB: I like that one! Erm… just make something up, but don't go too crazy.

Dom's Story

Domonnie Francis

Catering Supervisor

I'm a Catering Supervisor. I only started as agency staff in March 2022. I was from an agency company called Meridian before I got contracted with the Trust. I was a catering assistant.

There was another job role available in the Trust, which was the saffron supervisor, so I applied for that. Saffron is a big food ordering network system. You do your ordering on there. I was responsible for the wards mainly, patient's menus and ensuring the meals are corresponding with what's showing on the regular menu. The most important thing was to ensure all patients got a meal. And resolve any food or staff-related issues. I only did that role for six months and now I'm the catering supervisor.

I didn't have a huge passion for hospitals to be honest, but in all the jobs I've done, I've always done them to the best of my abilities. I always aim for greatness and to fulfil all my tasks in my job roles. I was doing other agency jobs, but it just wasn't working out for me. Sometimes our lives have to be completely shaken up, changed and rearranged to relocate us to the place we're meant to be. I decided to just give the hospital a shot because my missus told me about the hospital, so I applied. I was just thinking, it's just a job, I just need some money. So when they came to me and offered me a contract I was shocked – I spoke to other workers and they said, 'Oh, we waited two years for a contract, as an agency' and I was only there one month – so I took the offer. It was a great opportunity.

My English can be slightly broken. Sometimes, because I have to think about what I'm actually saying, so you can understand more. My country is an English-speaking country, but we have this other language, we call it Patois, it's the Jamaican Creole. We speak the Patois, mainly. It depends on how you were brought up. We don't speak the standard English on a daily basis, it's just our way of communicating with our friends or families back home and abroad.

The only reason why my English is this great is because in high school I found English quite fascinating. I liked writing stories. I had a friend from another school who always helped me with my English essays, grammatical errors, correct pronunciation and how to construct proper sentences. Also, my dad was a police officer. So he tried to correct me and my other brothers, like if we should come in and say something in 'Patwa' he would correct or tell us, to think about what was said and speak properly.

I was twenty-three when I left Jamaica. I had created a family for myself. I have a wife and two sons. I'd never dreamt I would come to the UK, but I got the opportunity to be with my family and also to achieve as many goals as I can and better my life.

Life in the UK is totally different from where am from, so I had to adapt and adjust.

I'm from Jamaica, Spanish Town, St Catherine. I grew up in a poor family and I thank God for that, because I learned how to be humble and appreciate everything. I came from nothing so mentally I never lose. Everything is a win or a lesson to me.

At the moment, being a supervisor can be challenging sometimes, staff think I'm the coolest supervisor they ever had because I don't really get upset. They've all been here for years you see so I expect them to actually know what to do without being supervised. They're all good people.

What I Know

Thomas Lee & Kim Moore

Domestic Assistant

I KNOW THE WAY from the train station
to the hospital

> I know how to direct people
> to any department in the hospital.

I still don't know my way to the canteen.

> I don't know how to get to Uppermill

I know what poems sound like.

> I know every colour code we have
> to use in the hospital

I know how to touch type.

> I know red is for toilets
> green is for kitchens/ward pantries
> blue is for wards/general areas
> yellow is for isolated areas

I don't know the names of all the catering staff yet

> I don't know every door code
> in the hospital

I don't know what that strange smell is

> I know that it's new carpet

I know how to eat cake

> I know how to cook seafood linguine

I know how to eat seafood linguine

> I know how to service my own car.

About the Project

UNTOLD STORIES OF THE NHS is a project led by Manchester Metropolitan University, funded by the Arts and Humanities Research Council (AHRC) and delivered in partnership with Lime Arts, NHS England, Manchester University NHS Foundation Trust and Manchester UNESCO City of Literature. In the organisation's 75th year, it celebrates the contribution of current and former NHS workers in a range of roles, reflecting on their working lives within the organisation and telling their stories through creative writing.

From January to May 2023, Manchester Metropolitan University poet Dr Kim Moore was Writer-in-Residence at Trafford General Hospital, the first NHS hospital to be opened, supporting staff to tell the story of their working lives within the NHS and produce their own creative writing. This book contains their NHS stories.

About Trafford General Hospital

The First NHS Hospital

The hospital now known as Trafford General was opened as Park Hospital in 1929. It was taken over by the War Department in 1939 and used first for British and then for American troops, hosting visits from boxer Joe Louis and from Glenn Miller and his band, who played to patients on the hospital's lawns. After the war, the hospital was handed back to Lancashire County Council, and on 5 July 1948, Park Hospital was re-opened by Health Minister Aneurin 'Nye' Bevan as the first hospital in the new National Health Service. Bevan welcomed the first NHS patient, Sylvia Diggory, and the hospital welcomed its first baby, Sandra Pook. Park Hospital became and has remained, in Bevan's own words, as recalled by Diggory, a physical monument to 'a milestone in history - the most civilised step any country had ever taken'. It was re-named Trafford General Hospital in 1988 and it is now part of The Manchester University NHS Foundation Trust, whose 10 hospitals deliver care to over 750,000 patients across Greater Manchester.

About the Editor

Kim Moore's pamphlet *If We Could Speak Like Wolves* was a winner in the 2011 Poetry Business Pamphlet Competition. Her first collection *The Art of Falling* (Seren 2015) won the Geoffrey Faber Memorial Prize. Her second collection *All The Men I Never Married* (Seren, 2021) won the 2022 Forward Prize for Best Collection. Her first non-fiction book *What The Trumpet Taught Me* was published by Smith/Doorstop in May 2022. She is a Lecturer in Creative Writing at Manchester Metropolitan University. A hybrid book of lyric essays and poetry *Are You Judging Me Yet? Poetry and Everyday Sexism* was published by Seren in March 2023.

List of Illustrations

The Univeristy would like to thank the following students from Manchester School of Art, who kindly produced the illustrations listed below:

Page xiv: Rebecca Horswill

Page 12: Ann Dinh

Page 30: Ann Dinh

Page 36: Lucy Waterworth

Page 40: Maria Hallewell-Pearson

Page 49: Ann Dinh

Page 50: Ann Dinh

Page 55: Rebecca Horswill

Page 68: Maria Hallewell-Pearson